ACID TRIP REPORT

WHAT IT'S LIKE TO TRIP ON LSD

ALEX GIBBONS

Copyright © 2020 by Alex Gibbons

All rights reserved.

No part of this book may be reproduced in any form or by any electronic or mechanical means, including information storage and retrieval systems, without written permission from the author, except for the use of brief quotations in a book review.

UPDATES

For a chance to go into the draw to win a FREE book every month like our 'Stoner Themed Coloring Book' (below), and other updates on our latest books, subscribe below!

https://psychedeliccuriosity.activehosted.com/f/1

For daily posts on all things Psychedelic, follow us on Instagram @Psychedelic.curiosity

Taking LSD was a profound experience, one of the most important things in my life

— STEVE JOBS

CONTENTS

Before We Begin ... ix
A little background on LSD/Acid ... xi

1. My First Low-Dose Acid Trip ... 1
2. I Tripped On Acid with My Wife ... 9
3. A Higher Than Expected Dose of LSD Leads To A Fun Trip ... 16
4. My LSD-Induced Spiritual Journey (1000 micrograms!) ... 26

FAQs ... 37
How to kill a trip - A Must have in a psychonaut's drug kit ... 45
Also by Alex Gibbons ... 53

BEFORE WE BEGIN

As we get started, we would like to say we are not trying to glorify the use of LSD/Acid or any other controlled substances. Drugs such as LSD can be harmful to you and sometimes to those around you also, so if you decide to use them, whether for fun, creative pursuits, or for spiritual purposes, the safety of you and those around you should be your most important consideration. The use of LSD should be a personal choice, and I don't try to sway you one way or the other.

I should also note that LSD is a controlled substance in most countries. Before you decide to purchase or carry around LSD, you should take the time to learn about any legal repercussions that you might have to contend with. If you make an informed decision to try out LSD, please ensure that you keep it out of reach of children.

As you will learn in these reports, LSD is a very strong substance, and even the smallest doses can have strong psychedelic effects. Therefore, it should be handled very cautiously and very seriously. Before you ingest it (or even touch it), ensure that you do enough research so as to prevent unexpected negative reactions.

Being a chemical substance, LSD is likely to interact with any prescription or over the counter drugs that you might be taking. So, before you use it, make sure that you understand the nature of any such interactions. You should also note that if you have any preexisting medical conditions, you may react differently to LSD than other people. If you have a chronic illness, it might be wise to avoid using LSD unless you are advised otherwise by a medical professional.

The stories in this book are meant to inform and to entertain you. These are first hand events by real people however we have changed the names and places to protect the privacy of the individuals.

It's also important to note that LSD trips are subjective; people tend to have different experiences depending on their state of mind, place and setting, and yours may be completely different to those described in this book.

A LITTLE BACKGROUND ON LSD/ACID

The acronym LSD stands for Lysergic Acid Diethylamide. It is a highly potent psychedelic substance that has been culturally influential for several generations. On the streets, LSD is also referred to as "Acid" or just "L". LSD and Acid are the same drug, and the two terms are used interchangeably. Not all substances marketed as LSD or Acid are pure Lysergic Acid Diethylamide however. Some dealers tend to concoct their own "designer drugs" by lacing LSD with other substances.

LSD was first discovered in the late 1930s, but its psychoactive effects were accidentally discovered by a Swiss chemist named Albert Hofmann in the 1940s. Hofmann had been working with LSD in his lab, when some of it got in contact with the skin on his fingertips. He started to hallucinate, and he was able to establish that the hallucinations were a direct result of the LSD crystals which were absorbed through his skin and into his bloodstream.

News of Albert's discovery spread fast, and by the 1950s, LSD was everywhere. It was studied by clinical researchers who hoped it would treat a myriad of mental health issues. Intellectuals thought it could make them sharper and the CIA also tested it, hoping to use it as a mind-control substance.

In the 1960s, the recreational use of LSD was very common, especially within the counterculture movement of that era. It wasn't until the early 1970s that LSD was reclassified as a controlled substance.

Fast forward to today: LSD is still commonly used for spiritual and recreational purposes. Additionally, as our society has become more liberal, the research into the medical applications of LSD has resumed. Scientists now believe that it can be used to treat addiction, alcoholism, and death anxiety (which is common among people with terminal illnesses).

LSD is so potent that its doses are measured in micrograms instead of grams. You need to ingest at least 15 micrograms of LSD to experience any effects. Doses of 75 micrograms and below are considered light. Doses of between 76 and 150 micrograms are common, especially among novice users of LSD. Doses of between 150 and 300 micrograms are strong, and those that exceed 300 micrograms are heavy.

Typical LSD trips last anywhere between eight and twelve hours, but in cases of heavy dosages, they can last a bit longer. The effects tend to kick in fifteen to thirty minutes after ingesting LSD, and they peak somewhere between three and five hours after the start of the trip.

LSD is typically ingested in the form of tabs. Tabs are small pieces of absorbent paper or fabric (e.g., blotting paper or gelatin sheets) that have been dosed with droplets of LSD. The paper can be placed on the tongue, below the tongue, or it can be swallowed. Drops of LSD solution can also be placed on pieces of candy to mask the taste. In some cases, LSD is sold in the form of tablets, capsules, or in liquid form.

1
MY FIRST LOW-DOSE ACID TRIP

I've always been curious about trying LSD. Most of my friends had already done it, and they all had interesting stories about divine revelations and ecstatic experiences. So, when I had my birthday party at a hotel, I figured that it would be a great time to take my first trip.

I was in the company of lots of friends, and in a familiar and safe environment, so I felt relaxed and comfortable in the hours leading to my trip. Still, I was very cautious because I didn't want to bite off more than I could chew; in terms of the intensity of the trip.

I decided to start out with a small dose of fifty micrograms. I had heard horror stories about novices trying out heavy doses all at once, only to have rapid adverse reactions. I waited a bit to see if there was any undesired effect. After about fifteen minutes, I was convinced that all was well, so I went on to up my dosage. In total, I ingested 150 micrograms worth of acid tabs. According to what I had learned from the internet and from friends, this was a fairly common dosage for first-timers.

The hotel had a nice streaming room, with massive screens and state of the art gaming setups. I was sitting on a couch in the room in between two of my friends when the LSD started to kick in.

On the main screen in the gaming room, they were replaying a video of the record-holding *Legend of Zelda: Ocarina of Time* Run by a famous gamer known as ZFG. I noticed the LSD was kicking in because the images on the screen were somehow starting to merge with my environment; the distinction between the two had begun to blur.

From my research on LSD, I had learned that the period between the moment you ingest LSD and the moment it kicks in, is very crucial in determining the nature of the trip that you'll end up having. As long as you were in a state of comfort and relaxation, you will be stress free once the effects kick in, so when I started to notice distortions in my visuals, I breathed a sigh of relief.

I started to notice that objects in my periphery were changing shape and color. Stationary objects were getting animated, but when I turned my head to look at them, they appeared normal once again. I also noticed as I moved my head, that it was lighter than usual. It felt like it was made of air, like it didn't have any weight at all.

In the beginning, the LSD trip felt sort of like a marijuana high, except that there was something strange about it, something I couldn't put my finger on. But, as it started to get stronger, the difference became more distinct. I felt like a plane that had just lifted off the ground. I was not living in reality anymore. Sure, the room around me looked the same, but suddenly, everything seemed to pop. All things were brighter and full of life.

Since my head had become virtually weightless, I wanted

to test my torso to see if it felt the same. I leaned forward from the sofa and gazed at the floor. However, my stream of thought was disrupted the second I noticed the peculiar appearance of the floor.

The carpeted floor had completely transformed, and now it looked like it had weird worm-like creatures crawling all over it. The patterns on the fabric seemed to form three dimensional mazes that were in a constant state of change. Some shapes would crawl into each other and merge into more complex shapes before disintegrating and starting all over again. If I hadn't been sure that the tabs I had taken were in fact LSD tabs, this would have confirmed it: Many people who have shared their LSD stories online have reported changes in the visual appearance of the floors.

As I lifted my gaze from the floor, I noticed that similar patterns were starting to form over everything else in the room. There were shapes and odd patterns creeping all over the walls. After admiring the walls for a while, trying to make sense of the animated pattern, I decided to shift my focus back to the screen again.

As I turned around, it felt as though my ears were turning much slower than the rest of my head. There was a distinct gap in cognition between my sense of hearing and my sense of sight. It seemed like I could see images first, and then the sound followed later, at a somewhat sluggish pace. It happened every time I tried to move my head around. The audio itself seemed distorted too, as the sound from the TV oscillated between being unusually deep, to being strangely hollow.

As I mentioned, I've smoked marijuana before, so I can't help but compare my LSD trip to my weed high. The most notable difference between the two experiences has to do with brain fog. When I was high on weed, I felt hazy, as though my mind was clouded by a heavy fog that kept me from thinking clearly. However, when I was on LSD, I felt completely sober and clear headed; there was no fog whatsoever; in fact, I felt as though my mind was sharper; more attentive. My senses felt like they had been heightened, and I was convinced that I was picking up on things that I ordinarily would have missed. I knew that I was under the influence of a mind-altering substance, but it did not feel that way at all.

I saw all sorts of things that I logically knew weren't real, but I felt I was in total command of all my faculties. LSD, it seemed, was not the kind of drug that "took over" and made you do things you had no intention of doing. Instead, it was the kind that opened you up and let you perceive things in a way you never imagined.

In a few minutes, someone turned off the main screen, and we all left the gaming room. We stood by the door for a while, exchanging greetings with another group that was coming into the room.

That's when I realized that LSD also had the effect of distorting people's appearances. When I held eye contact with the people I was talking to, their faces seemed slightly cartoonish. Their facial features seemed more pronounced. Their eyes seemed to have richer colors, and their facial expressions were more noticeable.

We went back into our hotel room, and I was relieved when I finally got to lie on my bed. The room had a calming and laid-back aesthetic, which I found rather relaxing. I thought that since there was less visual stimulation in the room, I had a better chance of experiencing something deeper. We just hung around and chatted for a while. The entire time, everything around me seemed to be in a constant state of motion. Some things looked like they were drifting towards me, but when I took a closer look, they again seemed to drift in the opposite direction. It was like there was an abundance of energy that kept all things vibrant.

As I lay flat on my back, head against my pillow, I started staring at the ceiling. It was white with a textured surface and repeated shapes in a grid pattern. It looked as though the patterns were rhythmically moving into each other and then back out again. I soon realized that the movements of the ceiling patterns were in sync with my own breathing.

As the conversation died down, I took my phone out and unlocked the screen. I wanted to check if there was anything interesting on my twitter feed. As soon as the screen came on, I was taken aback by the strange beauty of the phone. The light coming off the screen was brighter than I'd ever seen it. As I tried to focus my eyes, the light turned into all the colors of the rainbow, and everything started swirling around on the screen.

In the midst of the swirls, I managed to locate the twitter app, and I clicked on it. The letters that appeared on the screen moved up and down in a wave pattern. It was like the phone was a living organism, and the texts on the screen were either organs or blood vessels, pulsating to the rhythm of the sounds around the room.

After fixating on the letters for I while, I scrolled down my twitter feed, and that only seemed to agitate the letters further; they were now dancing vigorously as they rushed past. I decided that reading tweets at this time probably wasn't a good idea, so I put my phone away.

One of my friends suggested that we should do something more fun, so we elected to go back to the gaming room, which was now less crowded. We played video games for a while. I felt that the audio and visual stimulation was intense and overwhelming, but I decided to push through. I made a conscious effort to stay level headed, and with time, I was able to relax and enjoy the game.

Later, we heard about a party that was going on in another room, and we decided to crash it. There were at least a dozen people in the room. I felt more social and outgoing than I ordinarily do. I'm usually nervous about chatting up people I've never met before, but while on LSD, total strangers felt like old friends.

I felt like I had gained the ability to naturally understand the complex social dynamics that were at play in that room. I could immediately tell who likes who, and who didn't get along. I'm usually clueless about such things, but at that moment, I felt like a seasoned mentalist.

When I talked to people, I could automatically tell by their tone and their mannerisms, whether they were honest, real, or pretentious. It's like everyone's verbal and nonverbal cues were somewhat amplified, and no one could hide his or her true nature from me. If someone used coded language, I could immediately decipher it and understand the motivation behind their choice of words. Nothing seemed to get past me.

I had spent a lot of time researching about LSD, and I learned that lots of people tend to experience things like deep introspection, a sense of oneness with nature, spiritual fulfillment, or even ego death. So, whenever I could, I tried to empty my mind, to open myself up to the experience, in the hope that I too would have a taste of such an experience. However, none of that happened to me.

Sure, I had a few random thoughts that I thought were profoundly deep, but nothing concrete or groundbreaking.

Perhaps it was because I took such a small dose of LSD, or maybe it was because I spend most of the time in the distracting company of friends rather than in solitude – or maybe it was a combination of both reasons.

In retrospect, I think I'm glad that I didn't have any deeply personal or spiritual experiences during that trip. I was in the company of friends, most of whom were totally sober the entire time; that would hardly have been the right place and time to confront my inner demons. I took the acid because I wanted to have a great time. I certainly would have been a drag during my own birthday party if my trip had turned into a journey of self-discovery.

After interacting with strangers at the party in the other hotel room, my friends and I went back to our own suite. I was several hours into the trip, and I felt that there wasn't much to look forward to anymore. So, I went to bed. I put on my headphones, turned on the music, turned off the bedside lamp, and tried to fall asleep.

The music sounded hyperreal – like it was playing inside my brain, not just in my ears. Even though I was playing the kind of music that normally soothes me and helps me fall asleep, this time around, the music was sort of working me up. It was overly stimulating, so I decided to turn it off altogether.

When I closed my eyes, I realized that the LSD hadn't worn off as much as I thought. Colorful patterns started to form in my eyelids. They would start as small specs, grow in size at a rapid rate, disintegrate, and disappear into the periphery, leaving small specs that would go through the same process all over again.

What's more, I could hear music, even though the room was mostly silent. It seems that my ears were picking up sounds from the background and magnifying them so that it sounded like the sources were right there next to me.

Because of all the auditory and visual stimulation, it got really difficult for me to fall asleep. I fidgeted in bed for hours, with random thoughts rushing through my head. I must have eventually fallen asleep at some point because the next thing I remember was waking up the next morning. I didn't recall dreaming or having any nightmares.

As I woke up, I noticed that I was experiencing mild residual effects of the LSD. All the visual and auditory effects were gone, but I could still feel my mind was sharper, and the colors were brighter. As the day went by, things slowly returned to normal. I did not have any unusual come-down effects. In fact, the LSD just slowly and steadily faded away. Sometime in the afternoon, it just occurred to me that I was stone-cold sober.

2
I TRIPPED ON ACID WITH MY WIFE

My wife and I made the decision as a couple to try out LSD. We had heard so much about Acid from our friends, and we had been curious about it for a while. We have always enjoyed nature, and we figured that perhaps LSD would heighten our appreciation of the environment around us. So, we scored some LSD, cleared our respective schedules for the day, and we each ingested 350 micrograms of acid in tab form.

We stayed in the house for the first part of the trip, and listened to music. The come up seemed slower than we expected, but it was generally pleasant and enjoyable. As the acid started to kick in, the music became more vibrant, and for a moment, we just lay on the sofa, chilling and relaxing.

We live near the beach, so our plan was to go and hang out there when the acid kicked in. We decided to leave earlier than planned, so we could stop by a nearby pizzeria, pick up a box of pizza, and take it to the beach with us. When we got to the beach, we found a nice isolated place, spread the towel that my wife had around her waist over the sand,

and sat down, placing the pizza box between us. I leaned back and looked up into the sky, and that's when I realized that the first stage of my trip was in full swing.

I immediately noticed that the sky was moving rhythmically. It was like a massive living organism that was breathing heavily. "Does the sky look alive to you?" I asked my wife. She turned her gaze to the sky, and there was this awe-stricken look on her face.

I looked up again, this time squinting my eyes, trying to make out the details in the sky above. I noticed that there were airplanes all over the place. Some flew in straight lines, others in wavy lines, and others in circles. Some of them flew upwards, becoming smaller, until they just vanished. Others seemed to be in collision paths, but as they got closer to each other, they would either change directions or merge to form bigger planes. I tried to follow a particularly weird-shaped plane with my eyes, but it drifted so far up, that I thought it might have gone into space. I was transfixed by the absurdity of the whole display. I knew, logically, that there is no way that so many planes would fly so close to each other, but the visual images were so vivid that I felt conflicted.

Then, I accidentally stumbled upon an interesting realization. I saw one airplane that wasn't especially shapely, and I thought, "I wish that one would disappear." And just as the thought occurred to me, the plane vanished instantly. I realized that I had control over the planes in the sky! I tried the same thing with another plane and Poof! That one too, was gone. So, I turned it into a game. I would spot airplanes that I didn't like, and I would make them disappear, with the power of my mind; it was really fun, even though I knew they weren't real planes.

Shifting my attention from the imaginary planes, I realized

that there were portions of the sky that seemed to extend infinitely. Staring at one such part of the sky was like looking into a blue vertical tunnel. It was wide at the bottom, and it narrowed down as it went upwards. It wasn't really enclosed – its sides looked more like spirals than a continuous solid border. No matter how hard I squinted, I couldn't see where it ended; it just seemed to continue on and on, like some sort of portal from a science fiction movie.

It felt as though I was experiencing the hidden beauty of the world for the very first time. I've admired the sky so many times in my life, but this was the one time it seemed truly divine.

I realized that I was listening to music. This was no ordinary music though; it seemed to come from within me; conceived and performed inside my mind. And yet it was real and inspired. It sounded like a song I had known all my life, my favorite song of all time. It was so beautiful that my first instinct was to share it with the entire world.

I have always believed in the power of positive thought, and I've always had the conviction that as long as my intentions are pure, the thoughts that I put out in the universe will bear fruit. Given what had just happened with the imaginary planes, my belief in the power of thought had been affirmed, so I tried to use it to spread my song around.

I closed my eyes, put myself in a meditative state, focused my mind, and sent out the most powerful thought I could summon: "Share this awesome music with the world!"

I was amazed. Just as I sent out the thought, I started to see lights that were flickering on and off to the rhythm of my music. My darkened field of vision was suddenly populated with flashing lights of all colors of the rainbow, and I felt like I was in one of those raves where lights are programmed to pulsate to the beat of the music.

I couldn't tell if this magnificent music concert was a projection of my conscience, or it was the creation of some mysterious beings. Either way, I felt grateful, and I wished that I could prolong that moment and make it last for days. However, it was starting to get cold outside, and my wife tapped me on the shoulder and asked if we could get back to the house.

I would have loved to stay outside for longer, but my wife was right, the weather was starting to change, and we definitely would have been more comfortable indoors. In all that time, I hadn't even touched the pizza. I decided to have a couple of slices as we walked back home.

When we got home, I realized that my stomach was tensing up. I dashed into the nearest bathroom, and I threw up. My wife didn't seem to have any stomach issues, even though she had taken the same amount of LSD, and she had eaten more of the pizza that I had. The vomiting part was unpleasant, but I was determined to have a great experience, and I wasn't going to let it put me down.

After I freshened up, I entered into what I believe was the second phase of my trip. My visual hallucinations became very intense. Everything I looked at was so vibrant that I started getting overwhelmed. I decided to lay down for a bit, just to center myself again. As I lay with my back on the sofa, the brightness of the chandelier made me put my arm over my eyes: that's when I stumbled upon another amazing realization.

In a reflexive attempt to block the bright light, I waved my hand over my eyes, and I clearly saw that my hand had left a trail on its path. It was such a glorious thing to watch. I waved my hand across my face, this time intentionally, and there it was again. The trail was shaped like a series of hands. It immediately reminded me of the popular depiction of the Hindu goddess Shiva, where she seems to have multiple arms on both sides of the body. I waved my hand a few more times for fun, until my attention was drawn by the music that my wife had put on the stereo.

The music was upbeat, and I immediately felt a surge of energy inside me the moment it came on. I wanted to dance, and so did my wife. Now, I've always been shy about dancing. It's not that I have no interest in it; it's just that I have always believed myself to be a terrible dancer, and I thought that dancing would only result in embarrassment.

However, under the influence of LSD, it didn't matter; I was going to dance, and nothing would stop me. I started dancing, jumping up and down, playing air guitar, and making a bunch of crazy gestures. My wife danced next to me. First, she tried to follow my lead, then she decided that it was futile, and she too started dancing randomly.

As I danced, I felt as though I was surfing on this strong wave of energy; a wave so powerful that it lasted for hours. I really can't tell exactly how long we were dancing. We would only stop to yell and high-five each other when the song changed; then we would get back to business. I'm sure if any stone-cold sober person walked into the living room, they would have thought that we were totally crazy. It wouldn't have mattered to us anyway; this was the most fun thing we had done in ages.

Going into the trip, I had hoped that I could experience ego-death. I had learned that it involved losing awareness of your own body, and instead, perceiving yourself as an entity, or a freed spirit. I knew that in order to accomplish this, I had to be in a pure state of mind. So, throughout the trip, whether I was admiring the sky or dancing around, I was trying my best to think about peace, love, and enlightenment.

I tried to imagine myself shaking away all the negative things in my life. I pictured negativity, hatred, depression, and all other impurities that had clung to my soul, fall off as I danced vigorously.

I can't say that I experienced ego death, as described by many other users of LSD. I can, however, say that I managed to let go of negative things that had been weighed on me for years. It might not be a profound spiritual experience, but at least it's something.

At some point, I got tired of dancing, so my wife and I decided to test out our respective abilities to concentrate while under the influence of LSD. We had read about people claiming to develop telekinetic or telepathic abilities when tripping on acid, so we thought it would be fun to try and discover our "powers." We played a few guess games. For example, she would hold her hand behind her back, and she would telepathically tell me how many fingers she was holding up. I in turn, would say the number out loud. Generally, I was right about 40 percent of the time. I believe the percentage would have been higher if I had just trusted my instincts the whole time.

Afterward, I laid down on the couch and stared at the ceiling. I thought about the nature of reality. "We all take things at face value, but our reality is an illusion." I thought. "We just accept the fate that we have been dealt, but what if there is more?"

I found myself lost deep in thought, and it occurred to me

that most people have no clue what consciousness really is. It's important to understand it because it is what defines us. Consciousness is not the body – it transcends the body. The body, which we view as the thing that defines us, is actually just a vessel that contains our consciousness. That is why our reality is built on a lie.

It is our body that keeps us from communing with nature, from being one with the trees in the forest. Because of our gigantic egos, we have convinced ourselves that we are the most important species of all living creatures. To find the answers we are looking for, we need to look inside, not outside. We need to resolve the conflict within us, not to initiate conflict with other people, countries, or religions.

As these thoughts coalesced in my head, I could feel myself get right on the edge of letting go of my ego, but I never crossed the threshold. Instead, I started getting the sense that the LSD was slowly wearing off. The visuals were slowly dissipating, and I could feel reality slowly set in once again.

In the tail end of my trip, I resolved to meditate more, so that I could get used to opening myself up to spiritual experiences in the future. I certainly will try a higher dosage of LSD when I get the chance because I still want to go further; to have a profound spiritual experience.

3

A HIGHER THAN EXPECTED DOSE OF LSD LEADS TO A FUN TRIP

It all started about a couple of months before the actual trip. My friend kept talking about his acid trip, and he mentioned that he had a few LSD tabs to spare. I decided to buy four tabs from him, each containing 110 micrograms of LSD. They were clean white square tabs with no branding at all. As he sold them to me, he warned me to be extremely careful with them since they were extraordinarily powerful. I dismissed that last part because I thought that's what a good pusher would say about his product.

My trip was on a Saturday. I was hanging out in my college dorm room in the middle of the morning with nothing to do. I didn't have any plans for the weekend. Saturday mornings are usually dull times on campus because of the after-effects of the Friday night parties. Most of my friends were either too hungover to do anything fun, or they were still passed out. I remembered my LSD stash, and I figured it would be a great time to take one tab.

Now, I had tripped at least a handful of times before, both on LSD and mushrooms. I had grown fairly accustomed to the horrible taste of the tabs, so I didn't think much of it when I took one tab out of the carefully locked bag, placed it on my tongue, gurgled around for a while, and finally swallowed it.

Now it was time to wait for the effects to kick in. I figured that it wouldn't take more than twenty five minutes for me to start feeling something. However, after waiting for about thirty five minutes, I felt nothing. I kept waiting. With each passing minute, I grew more suspicious of my friend, who had sold me the tabs. He was always a smooth talker, and I wouldn't put it past him to exaggerate the concentration of his product in order to make more money. The fact that the tabs lacked any labels only served to compound my suspicions: Sure, it was LSD, I could recognize that taste anywhere; but could it have been a smaller dose than advertised?

After forty five minutes with no reaction, I concluded that my friend had duped me, and I decided to take the three remaining tabs all at once. I swallowed them fast. Now that I believed they were small doses, my hope was that they'd add up, and I would at least experience a decent reaction.

Five minutes after I had ingested the last three tabs, I started to feel something. The first tab was kicking in, and as it turns out, it wasn't under-dosed. It just took a hell of a long time to enter my system. I realized that I had stumbled upon a slow-reacting batch of LSD, and I had confused it for an under-dosed one, my original plan was to have a 110 microgram trip, but because of my impatient and suspicious nature, I had taken the entire 440 microgram stash.

For the next forty five minutes, I enjoyed the come-up of the first dose. I experienced mild visual hallucinations, and I felt warm energy coming from within, which kept me cheerful the entire time.

At least one and a half hours after taking the first tab, roughly fifty minutes after taking the other three, I started to experience the full effects of all the 440 micrograms that were in my system. In my previous trips, I had been keen on limiting my doses, and my highest one so far had been about 150 micrograms. I had experienced slight hallucinations, mostly related to my breathing pattern and some closed eye visuals. Now, I was in unchartered territory.

I like to move around when I'm tripping. I know lots of people who prefer to chill in their rooms, especially when under high doses of LSD, but I've always been outdoorsy. Besides, I didn't think 440 micrograms was too high a dose to render me incapable of being up and about. I grabbed my phone and put on my headphones. I found my favorite classic rock playlist, and I started playing it. I went out and just strolled around campus for a while.

As I walked about, my sense of time started to get really distorted. I felt like I was walking around for hours, but when I checked my phone, I realized that I had only been out for a few minutes. I started to think about time as a concept.

"Time," I thought, "couldn't possibly be from this dimension." It occurred to me that time was a relative concept, and it was therefore subjective. People experience time differently. For some, it moved fast, while for others, it moved much slower. I felt that for me, time was moving very fast, at a supernormal speed. Compared to me, time was slow for everyone else. "I must be from a different dimension!" I thought. "I'm from the same dimension as time! Why else would time move so fast for me?"

Now, that might sound nonsensical to a sober mind, but when I was tripping, I could swear that it was the most profound thought that I ever had. It was a neat theory that explained why fifteen minutes of my time felt like several hours.

Then I thought, "If I'm from the same dimension as time, what was it like there? Why am I here, in this foreign dimension? And what am I? Could I be an alien species, a superior one, perhaps?"

I had read a lot about the use of acid, and one belief that seemed common among many users was that LSD had the ability to open the portals of perception. Acid, I had learned, could reveal to you realities beyond anything you could imagine.

With the LSD in full swing, it felt to me that the portals of perception were now wide open. These weren't just portals; they were floodgates. My mind was flooded with hundreds of new ways to look at things. I couldn't keep my thoughts straight at all. When one stream of thought started to form in my conscious mind, ten other streams would emerge, seemingly from nowhere, and drown that one out. I started to get overwhelmed by the complexity of my own thoughts, and I felt I needed to focus on something in my immediate environment.

Looking straight ahead, I spotted a tree in the middle of the lawn off the pavement. As I kept approaching it, it started to morph before my very eyes. It changed both in shape and color. I felt drawn to the tree, so I decided to just observe it for a while. I spotted a park bench right nearby, and I walked over and sat there, facing the tree, which was now just a few paces away.

I admired the tree, as it contorted itself and changed its color, it was green for a second and then yellow, then orange, then red, then brown, then green again. This cycle kept repeating itself. It looked like some kind of magical tree out of a fairy tale or some fantasy story, like the kind of tree that would either grant your wishes or point you to your destination. I kept looking for a face, or any humanoid features, but there weren't any. I just sat there for a while, staring in awe as the tree performed its act.

As I sat on the bench, I started to realize that the music had become a part of me. Initially, it was clear to me that the music was coming from my earphones, but somewhere along the way, without me noticing it, I had somehow merged with the music, and now I was one with it. The song filled me from head to toe and seemed to be a form of energy that pulsated and surged within the cells in my body. It was in sync with all my movements. I was the one singing the lyrics and playing all the instruments. This was a truly powerful and beautiful feeling.

After enjoying being one with the music for a while, I felt I needed to experience something else, perhaps with some company. I decided to call my friend, the same one who sold me the LSD. I felt I needed to talk to someone who wouldn't be judgmental about my use of a mind-altering substance, and he was the first person I thought about. When I couldn't reach him on the phone, I called another friend; this one wasn't into psychedelics, but he was still one of the most open-minded friends I had. He picked up the phone, and when I asked him to come and hang out, he informed me that he couldn't drive over because he was high on weed.

When I told him that I had accidentally taken a higher dose of LSD than I had planned, he said, "Dude, that sounds epic! Just ride it out and see where it takes you."

We kept talking on the phone for a while, but there was a lot of foot traffic around, and I was getting distracted by all the visual and auditory stimuli, so I decided to leave the park bench and go into a nearby lecture hall, which was empty at the moment.

When I got to the lecture hall, there were fewer distractions there, but then I was presented with a new problem. I started to forget that my friend on the phone was actually another person, a separate entity from me. It sounded as though he was a voice in my head. I kept providing telepathic responses to him, instead of saying them out loud, and that made for an awkward conversation.

At least twice, he had to say, "Dude, are you still there?" to get me to offer verbal responses. I realized that the conversation was becoming futile, so we both agreed to hang up and catch up some other time.

At the moment, it was about three and a half hours since I took the first tab. I decided to go back to my dorm room and do some drawing. I have always heard about great painters and artists who used LSD to spark creativity, and I wanted to see if I might be able to do something similar. When I got to my room, I grabbed some plain papers from my table and went to the lounge.

I sat down and started drawing. I immediately realized that I hadn't brought my colored pencils with me, so I tried to make do with the ordinary ones. I intended to draw a curving pathway that was lined with trees. It would narrow down towards the horizon, and it would be framed by a rainbow as it wound its way towards the top of the paper. I outlined the winding pathway, and then I went back to my room and brought some colored pencils for drawing the vegetation and the rainbow.

I worked on my drawing for the better part of an hour. The visual image in my head was very vivid, but it didn't translate onto the paper. It turns out that the LSD couldn't turn me into Picasso. The end result was as horrible as anything else I had ever drawn.

My dorm mates started coming into the lounge. They started chatting me up. A couple of them came up to me and noticed that I was acting a bit odd. They immediately realized that I was tripping because I had gained a bit of a reputation for using psychedelics. Many of them were my friends, and I knew for a fact that most of them were open to experimenting with mind-altering substances, so I wasn't worried that I would end up in trouble.

One of my dorm mates told me that my pupils were so large that my eyes looked cartoonish. Hearing that, a bunch of other guys came over to look at my eyes, and they all seemed to agree that they looked a bit weird. Someone started a debate on the use of LSD, and everyone else chimed in.

The discussion went on for about an hour. There were those who thought that LSD was dangerous, but many of them said they'd try it at least once. I realized that even though they were smart, well informed, and open-minded, a lot of my friends seemed to have internalized the negative propaganda that they heard about LSD. I tried my best to dispel some of their misconceptions, and I shared some of my experiences, both from the current trip and from past trips.

I described my visual hallucinations to my dorm mates. As I did that, they seemed to grow more vivid. The visuals were now taking over everything, and some of my dorm mates started looking weird. One of them seemed to have two sets of eyes, and another one looked like he had things crawling all over his body. Sometimes, I would talk in incomplete sentences as my train of thought would be distracted by particularly odd patterns that were emerging out of my peripheral vision.

At some point, I stopped explaining things to my friends and instead started asking questions that seemed to astonish them. I shared my earlier theory about time, and one of them said: "He's turning into Einstein." In retrospect, I'm not sure if that was a compliment or a sarcastic comment, but at the moment, I totally believed that he was praising me, and it boosted my confidence.

We had been talking for a while when the resident advisor walked in and found us right there in the lounge. She had always been the friendly type, so she joined us. We quickly changed the topic of conversation, but I suspected that she might have heard something about LSD. I started to freak out. I thought that even though she was cool, she might feel obligated to do something if she knew that I was on drugs. She came over and sat on the armrest of the sofa that was adjacent to the one I was on.

"What are we talking about?" she asked.

"We are just chilling," someone said as some of the other guys started bringing up random topics, in a clear attempt to cover for me. I kept silent because I thought I would be exposed if I said anything.

As everyone kept talking and laughing, my nervousness started affecting my visual hallucinations. Suddenly, it looked like everything, and everyone was covered with eyes that were staring at me. First, the eyes were subtle, lurking in the background. However, with time, they started to get more and more prominent. They also seemed to be widening, and that really disconcerted me. I knew right then that I needed to get the hell out of there.

I bought some time, and then, as casually as I could, I got up and said: "I have some stuff to do in my room."

I slowly walked away, trying to avoid arousing suspicion. I felt like the smartest person in the world after successfully getting out of that situation. However, in hindsight, I think the resident advisor really knew that I was on drugs, and she just let it slide. Some of my dorm mates later told me that she had caught a few people with joints before, but she never reported them.

When I got to my room, I found my roommate had come back, and he was playing some music on his laptop. We talked for a while, as my nervousness dissipated.

At least seven hours into the trip, another close friend sent me a message asking if I wanted to spend the evening snowboarding. "Hell yeah!" I texted back. He promised he would come over in about half an hour. I had bought some pineapple slices for a trip-time snack earlier on, so I ate them as I waited for him to show up.

My friend arrived thirty minutes later, right on schedule. He called me downstairs, and off we went, driving down the twilight road. When we hit the highway, the streetlights looked so awesome. It was like we were hurtling through space in a ship, and the lights were stars and planets, flying past us.

I was starting to come down a bit, and I felt I had regained adequate control over my body, so I was certain that snowboarding wouldn't be dangerous at this point.

We go to the summit, and we left the car and geared up. I put on my earphones, turned the music to max volume and then we snowboarded down the mountain. The feeling was unlike anything I had experienced before. I felt like I was flying, like a jet fighter, to the soundtrack of 'Rap God' by Eminem. I've never felt more alive.

We snowboarded for at least three hours before we got too tired and decided to drive back to campus. On the way back, I realized that my LSD trip was over for the most part. All those profound thoughts I had throughout the day were now gone, and my body felt completely normal. I realized that I was really hungry, as I had not had a proper meal throughout the day.

Some minor visual elements stayed with me for a bit. They made it difficult for me to fall asleep, but other than that, nothing interesting happened after I got back to my dorm. I finally fell asleep a few minutes past three am.

In general, I think it was a great experience. I would say it was mostly recreational, and not at all spiritual. I was worried about taking such a high dosage, but in the end, 440 micrograms of LSD turned out to be pretty manageable for me.

If you're interested in trying out LSD, I would recommend it, but I would suggest that you start out with a small dose. Be patient if you think the come-up is taking too long because it seems that the timing differs from batch to batch. Don't make the same mistake I did; although mine turned out well, I still think it is better if you only take the dose for which you are mentally prepared for.

4

MY LSD-INDUCED SPIRITUAL JOURNEY (1000 MICROGRAMS!)

I have been on LSD trips before, so this time around, I decided to up the game and trip on a heavy dose of roughly 1000 micrograms. I knew that this would be intense, and I wanted to reduce the risk of a bad trip, so I started getting myself ready at least a week before the trip.

One week before the trip, I stopped having coffee, and all other beverages that contain caffeine. I had learned through online forums that caffeine increases nervousness ever so mildly. Evidently, that nervousness can be magnified by LSD, leading to a bad trip.

To reduce my predisposition to anxiety, I stopped watching the news, as well as movies and TV shows with violent content. I also did the best I could to avoid spending time with the toxic people in my life. I really didn't want any negative news or upsetting thoughts lurking at the back of my mind as I went into this trip.

Instead of watching TV, I decided to spend the entire week reading spiritual books that could relax me and lift my spirits. I mostly focused on texts about Buddhism and the spiritual experiences of influential gurus such as Alan Watts.

A couple of days before the trip, I stocked up on snacks. I didn't want to have to leave the house for any reason during the trip, because I would be on a heavy dose of LSD. I bought some ice-cream, candy, peaches, and salty crackers.

On the day of the trip, I decided to take a nap for a few hours before ingesting the LSD. I felt I needed extra mental energy for the trip, so even though I had slept just fine the night before, I thought a bit of rest would do me some good.

I woke up from my nap, about five hours before the trip, feeling rather famished. I poured myself a bowl of cereal with milk, and I had a glass of orange juice as well. When I was done with the meal, I did all my chores because I really wanted to get things out of the way, so I could remain focused during my trip. I chopped my peaches into little bits, and I made sure all my other snacks were ready and easily accessible.

At this point, I only had an hour before the trip, so I put on some relaxing tunes, and I got myself into a meditative mood. With a few minutes to go, I stood up and did a few stretching and breathing exercises, just to relax and to dissipate some of the tension that was building up inside. It was now time to drop some LSD.

I'm twenty years old, and I weigh 165 pounds (roughly 75 kilograms). When it comes to the use of mind-altering substances, I wouldn't call myself a light-weight. Still, I knew that today's dosage would not be a walk in the park for me.

I took 4 tabs containing 220 micrograms each, and 1 tab

containing 110 micrograms of LSD; that's a total of 990 micrograms in one go. These were high-quality pure LSD tabs, and they were from the same batch that some friends of mine had recently tripped on. I put a couple of the tabs below my tongue, and the rest on top. They had a somewhat disgusting taste and texture. For several minutes, I tried swishing saliva around my mouth, hoping that the tabs would dissolve faster than usual.

I was sitting on my bed, holding my laptop, trying to record my experience in as much detail as I could. Twenty minutes after taking the tabs, they were still in my mouth, undissolved and uncomfortable, with a horrible taste. I got annoyed with them, and I decided to just flush them down with a glass of water.

After swallowing the tabs, the disgusting taste still lingered on my tongue, but it was milder. I was already starting to feel the effects of the LSD. I started to have this sensation that I was sinking into my bed. Although I knew that I was sitting still, it felt like my bed was this thick cloud, and I just kept going deeper into it, as it kept engulfing me with comfort and warmth.

I checked the time on my laptop, and I realized that it was thirty minutes since I first put the tabs on my tongue. I looked up and gazed at the wall. The walls in my room usually have a dotted pattern. As I stared at the dots, they all started to change in form, turning into pictures. A part of the wall morphed into a picture of an ancient temple, and the dots seemed to form the outline of that temple. Another section of the wall turned into a forested area, filled with majestic trees and tendrils. The pictures weren't exactly full of color, but they were just vibrant enough for me to make out the specific details of the temple and the forest.

Roughly one hour after dropping LSD, I started to have this intense feeling, like all of my senses were starting to get heightened, and I could distinctly hear sounds over long distances. I could hear people outside my apartment having conversations; normally, I would only hear mumbling, but this time, I could make out every word they were saying.

Things around me started to feel very soft, as though they were losing their structural rigidity; my walls and the furniture looked like they were made of fluffy material instead of solid mass. Everything in sight was somehow broken down into its elementary colors.

At this point, I also started to lose my sense of time. I've tried to reconstruct the timeline to the best of my recollection but for the remainder of the story, the times I quote will be estimates.

I closed my eyes and tried to meditate but I was distracted by the awful taste in my mouth, which had changed slightly. Now I had this dry cardboard feeling on my tongue and throat. I took another gulp of water which soothed the sensation a little bit. I closed my eyes again, breathed as deeply as I could, and tried to relax some more.

Almost as soon as my eyes were shut, I went into this deep trance. Hundreds if not thousands of thoughts were rushing through my mind, and they all seemed like great and profound insights. It was as though the secrets of the universe were being revealed to me in quick and random progression. I cannot remember even a small fraction of those thoughts right now, but at the moment, I was absolutely certain of their profound nature.

In the midst of the trance, I realized that I had an unusual superpower. I could pretty much playback any song in my head, and it sounded as real as anything I have ever heard. I had turned off the music in my room before, so I'm completely sure that my mind wasn't contorting the sounds I heard in real life and making them seem like they were in my head.

It was mesmerizing to say the least: I had this ability to conjure up entire orchestras in my head, play complex pieces of music, and hit every single note in perfect harmony. I could distinctly hear every instrument in the orchestra. It felt like I was playing each instrument on my own and conducting the orchestra at the same time. I was the maestro, pianist, violinist, cellist, percussionist, and much more, all at the same time, and it was magical.

I must have stayed in the trance for about a couple of hours. When I opened my eyes, I felt totally lost in space and time. I had no idea where I was or what I was doing. I just sat there for another ten minutes, trying to figure out what was going on. I started to freak out a little bit. I felt like something was really off, or maybe I was going mad. I tried to calm down and examine my environment to make sense of what was going on.

It took me quite a while to remember that I was actually in my own room and that I had taken LSD. That realization calmed me down slightly, but I still felt very weird. It was as if my reality was gone. The entire paradigm in which I existed had vanished, and I was left there, with nothing concrete to define my world. It was as if I was floating in a world that had no particular rules or constructs, and that did not sit well with me.

I felt that it was up to me to chart my new reality; to make sense of this universe that I now inhabited. However, as soon as I found a system that made some sense, one that explained my reality and made my world cohesive, it would slip my mind, and I would have to start all over again. If you've never been on a drug-induced trip before, this would seem nonsensical to you, but I've come to learn that it's actually a common experience that is well documented by many people who have used psychedelics before.

At first, every time I failed in my attempt to make sense of my reality, I became increasingly frustrated. It can be disconcerting to any intelligent being, to exist in a world without understanding its rules. However, after a few fruitless attempts, I decided to stop trying to make sense of my reality, and instead to just go with it. As soon as I stopped digging for answers, I felt this overwhelming sense of relief, like a huge load had been taken off my mind. My brain had been tying itself in knots trying to define a place it didn't understand, but now it was letting loose, and switching to autopilot. That was one of the greatest feelings I've ever had.

As my worries subsided, I realized that the reason why my reality felt so different and strange was that my body wasn't part of me anymore. Somehow, I could not feel my body, and I was okay with it. It was like I wasn't a physical object, but a mind; a collection of thoughts, drifting around in a metaphysical dimension.

I was now at peace with my current state, so I decided to try meditating once more. I remembered the things I had read in the Buddhist books earlier; about letting go of the ego and the sense of self. Thanks to LSD, I was able to do that, and for a while, my mind was in a tranquil state.

Four hours into my trip, things started to get really crazy. So far, my eyes were shut, and I had seen objects within my field of vision. But at that moment, I started to feel as though I could really see through my tightly shut eyelids!

My mind was totally blank, and I sat there for what seemed like several days, experiencing things beyond my wildest imagination.

I had been meditating for sometime, so I couldn't tell exactly when it happened, but I found myself in the company of invisible enlightened Buddhist masters. I could feel their presence, and in my mind, I pictured them floating next to me in the lotus position. They were very calm, and I too mirrored their calmness, as if it was contagious. They kept telling me, in a humming voice, to have peace of mind.

I'm not very experienced in matters of spirituality. In fact, I consider myself a novice when it comes to meditation, but in the state that I was in, all I had to do was copy what the enlightened masters were doing.

I felt as though I was experiencing the entire universe all at once: Every person, animal and plant, every drop of water, and every grain of sand, every atom, and every object in space. It felt great to be one with everything. I wanted to stay in that state forever, but one of the enlightened Buddhist masters telepathically informed me that it could take a few hundred years for me to complete that experience in its entirety. The vast nature of the universe meant that we were unable to experience it all in one lifetime.

Since I couldn't experience the whole universe on my own, I wondered what it was like to do so, and I wanted to know if any of the Buddhist masters could describe it to me. As it turned out, they all had only experienced fractions of the universe, albeit bigger chunks than me. They however, told me that one person had, in fact, experienced the entire universe; the Buddha himself!

One of the masters went on to explain to me that the

Buddha knows all pleasures and pains that have or will ever exist because he took the time to experience the universe, and to be one with all things.

As I was still trying to wrap my mind around this revelation, the masters took me to what looked like a massive fort, and we stopped in front of the iron gates. They left me there, and I knew that I was supposed to knock on the gates and wait to see what comes next. But just as I was about to knock, a gigantic ghost-like humanoid opened the door.

I wanted to know where I was, but the giant humanoid anticipated my question, and with a smile, he told me that the fort was the repository of all knowledge.

As I stepped into the repository, I realized that I had the ability to fly, so I started using it, I flew around next to the giant ghost-like humanoid. He seemed to be walking, but thanks to his massive size and giant steps, we were able to keep abreast, even though I was flying at full speed. We got to a platform within the building, and I saw a very thick book neatly positioned at the center. "This," he said, "is the book of wisdom and knowledge."

As I admired the book, the giant humanoid moved to the other side of the elevated platform and opened it in my direction. I felt a strong energy emanating from the book and going into my brain, as though the information contained within it was being inscribed in my head. As this was happening, I could feel all the questions I've ever had being answered instantly. All the things I didn't understand before – things about the universe, about spirituality, and about life – they suddenly made perfect sense to me.

The experience is difficult to put in words. Because of the knowledge in that book, everything was clear to me now.

The world made perfect sense, and I realized that everything, good or bad, was exactly the way it's supposed to be; the way the universe intended. I should note that after my trip was over, I couldn't remember the answer to all the mysteries of the universe, but I swear, in that fleeting moment, I felt like every mystery was resolved. I don't know much about enlightenment, but I knew that I had experienced it, even if it did not last.

The book of wisdom and knowledge gave me the power of teleportation. I was able to jump from the fort into any place or time in the universe and to experience that place in a spiritual sense. I suddenly found myself darting back and forth, from place to place, taking in as much information as I could. Instead of experiencing these different places through my senses as I would in real life, I was able to take them in, like colorful beams of energy flowing through my spiritual eye and straight into my soul.

After a while, the giant humanoid put the book aside, and for the first time, I was able to pay close attention to the way he looked. It seemed to me that he was the embodiment of love and compassion. When I wanted to know who he was, he just put on a broad smile, but he didn't answer. I suspected that he might be the Buddha, but I got the sense that he didn't want to make our interaction about himself.

I asked the giant humanoid, "How do I achieve success in my spiritual and personal life?"

He grinned once more, and answered: "Watch for the signs!"

I'm not sure what that meant, but I decided from that point onwards, to be attentive and introspective so that I wouldn't miss any important signs.

Around seven hours into my trip, I stopped meditating, and I started becoming aware of my immediate surroundings. I realized that the LSD was starting to wear off. I also noticed that I was hungry. I got up from the bed, walked to the kitchen, and found the peaches that I had prepared earlier on. I quickly ate up the entire plateful.

At this point, I felt that it would be a great time to note down some of the things that I experienced during my trance and my meditation to avoid forgetting important details. I got a paper and a pen. But just as I was about to start jotting things down, I noticed that the lines and letters were jumping around on the page. When I paid close attention, I realized that they were actually dancing to the rhythm of my heartbeat!

By now, the sun was about to come up, and as I tried to meditate again, I could hear the birds chirping. In the distance, I could hear the humming sound of some sort of engine. The sounds weren't just random; they were somehow related to each other. It felt as though all creatures and machines out there were having a passionate conversation.

Nine hours into my trip, this overwhelming nauseous feeling started to creep up my throat, and I rushed to the bathroom as fast as I could. Unfortunately, it was too late. I barfed on the floor, and some of it got on my jumper. I felt really disappointed that this had happened, but as I was preparing to clean things up, I realized that the vomiting might not have been caused by the LSD; I ate my fruit in such a hurry, I forgot to chew properly.

As I cleaned the floor, I noticed that the tiles seemed to morph into fish-like blobs and swim around; I was still a little high.

For the remainder of my trip, I felt a mild buzz, the kind you would feel if you took a low dosage of LSD. I spent most of this time excitedly playing back the experiences that I had earlier, still amazed at the spiritual journey that I had taken.

Thirteen hours into the trip, all the visual hallucinations had stopped, although things still looked very bright and colorful. Throughout the next day, I felt like my senses were heightened, but the visual aspects of my trip were now permanently gone.

FAQS

How bad is acid for you?

Acid had both short-term and long-term effects that can pose serious risks to your health and safety.

Short-term negative effects of acid

Even small doses of LSD can cause:

- Visual effects (it makes colors seem brighter and more vivid; it blurs or distorts the appearance of objects or people; etc.)
- Changes in your mood (makes you euphoric, hyper-aware, anxious, blissful, confused etc.).
- Changes in the way you think (it can make you believe that time is moving faster or slower, or that you transcend reality; it can cause you to have strange insights, or scary thoughts).

While these psychoactive effects may be your reason for taking LSD in the first place, they may cause you to misjudge dangerous situations, and in extreme cases, that could result in death or injury.

Acid also has other short-term effects (apart from the psychoactive ones), that could cause underlying medical conditions to act up. For example, LSD can cause changes in your heart rate, blood pressure, body temperature, and pupil dilation.

There are also some minor short-term effects that could cause you some discomfort or just affect your ability to perform other activities. For example, LSD may cause weakness, tremors, numbness, dizziness, insomnia, sweating, reduced appetite, nausea, vomiting, or dry mouth.

LSD trips are unpredictable, and your current state of mind affects the nature of your trip. For example, if you are stressed, depressed, or have negative thoughts, you are more likely to have a bad trip.

In some cases, people have reported having bad trips that seemed like "living nightmares." They spend hours feeling paranoid, scared, and detached from their bodies and unable to find their way back. LSD has been known to cause both panic attacks and psychotic episodes in some users.

Studies have shown that life threatening physical reactions to LSD only occur when users take doses greater than 400 micrograms.

Long-term negative effects

LSD is not addictive in a strict medical sense. That means that users won't experience withdrawal symptoms when they stop using it. However, it can be "psychologically addictive" since it offers an escape from reality.

The human body develops a tolerance for LSD at a very fast rate; if the same dosage of LSD is taken for three days, back to back, no psychoactive effects will be experienced on the third day. The user would have to increase the dosage to feel any change.

When LSD is used consistently and excessively, it can cause long-term psychosis. It has also been known to trigger schizophrenia and other mental conditions, especially in people who are genetically predisposed to mental illnesses.

Even if you take LSD just once, you may experience flashbacks days after the effects have worn off.

Does Acid put holes in my brain?

NO. Acid does not put holes in your brain. This is a very popular myth that was started by anti-drug campaigners. The myth actually originated in the late 90s, and it was created to make young people afraid of taking ecstasy, but with time, it has come to be associated with all psychedelic substances, including LSD.

In fact, there are no chemical or biochemical substances that have the ability to put literal holes in your brain. That kind of brain damage is only possible if you receive a blow to the head through blunt force trauma.

Some people have pointed out that the "holes in the brain" myth is metaphorical and not literal. There's the common claim that LSD can cause your brain to be "permafried" (a non-medical term that means permanently damaged). That too is NOT true. Studies have consistently shown that using LSD once in a while for recreational purposes is unlikely to cause any kind of enduring brain damage.

You may experience occasional flashbacks (as we mentioned when we discussed the negative effects of LSD), but those are extremely rare, and they may cause slight distractions, but they won't keep you from functioning normally.

How long should you take between acid trips?

You should take a minimum of three days between LSD trips. As we've mentioned, taking LSD day after day will cause you to build a quick tolerance to the psychedelic.

When you take LSD for the first time, you develop a temporary tolerance to that dosage. That tolerance lasts for three days. On day four, your brain's tolerance will return to its baseline level.

We pointed out earlier that if you take LSD for three consecutive days, you develop a permanent tolerance; effectively, that means that the concentration you take for those three days will become your new baseline, so in future, you would have to take a higher dose to feel anything.

If you trip on a particularly heavy dose of LSD, you might want to wait up to seven days before taking LSD again.

Can you take too much acid?

Yes you can take too much acid. It's possible to overdose on LSD. Although there are no confirmed incidences of people dying as a result of overdosing on acid, there are lots of well documented negative effects that have resulted from the ingestion of too much LSD.

There are records of people who snorted lines of LSD after confusing it with cocaine (remember LSD is so powerful that its dosages are only measured in micrograms). In these instances, there were reports of respiratory difficulties, stomach and intestinal bleeding, hyperthermia, and in some cases, people ended up in comas. If this were to happen to someone and he/she didn't receive immediate medical attention, it's possible that he/she could die.

If you use LSD, whether it's for recreational or spiritual reasons, by all means, do not exceed the 1000 microgram dose. Leave those extreme doses for highly experienced shamans.

What should I do to help someone having a bad trip?

Anyone can experience a bad LSD trip, no matter what precautions they take in preparation for the trip. When someone is having a bad trip there are several things that you can do to help them weather the storm.

There is a common belief that Vitamin C (fruits and juices) can treat bad LSD trips, but that has been debunked as a myth. Still, if the person having the bad trip believes this myth, Vitamin C could have a placebo effect on them, so it might actually be helpful to offer them a glass of fruit juice or some fruit slices.

You can also help someone who's having a bad trip by constantly reminding him/her that the hallucinations are not real. LSD can distort a person's reality, and some hallucinations may appear to be hyper-real, but the fact is that the person will still have the mental awareness to understand what you are saying, especially if you repeat it over and over. Talking to the person in a firm and calm voice can really help to ground them.

You can also help someone by trying to stay connected with them, so that they aren't lost in their visual and auditory hallucinations. Ask the person to describe to you what they are seeing, hearing, or feeling.

As you try to connect with the person, avoid behaving in ways that would overwhelm him/her. Don't raise your voice, and don't bring other people into the room; for a person having a bad trip, having too many people try to help at the same time can actually make things worse.

You should also make sure that the person stays safe. If someone is having a bad trip, there is an increased risk that he/she could walk into traffic, accidentally fall from a great height, or stumble into some other hazard. You should make sure that you help the person stay in a safe and familiar place. Try to keep the person in his own living room or bedroom, and avoid kitchens. A good rule of thumb is, don't let them do anything you wouldn't trust a toddler to do.

By all means, do not let the person self-medicate in any way. A person having a bad trip may want to take sleeping pills, pain killers, alcohol, or even some more LSD to change their current state. Keep all these things away from them. Some of these substances may make things worse.

You should also try your best to ensure that the person's physical needs are taken care of. A person having a bad trip will be too preoccupied to eat, stay hydrated, or rest. Try to get them to eat something light. There is a possibility that the person may be having a bad trip because his/her blood sugar is low, and it's affecting his/her mood. Drinking lots of fluids may also help to flush the LSD out of the persons system a lot faster.

The person is likely to be restless, but it might help to get him/her to lie down on a sofa or a bed. If he/she needs to go to sleep but is unable to, you could play some soothing music, preferably something of his/her own playlist.

If things really get out of hand, and the person becomes

physically ill, you could be dealing with a contaminated batch of LSD. In such cases, you need to call an ambulance, or to take the person to an emergency room.

Many people are afraid of seeking medical help, or offering up important details to medical personnel in case of drug-related emergencies because they are afraid of having to deal with the law. The fact is that in most jurisdictions, it's unlikely that the person would be arrested just for having drugs in his/her system (possession is a different story). Feel free to tell the doctors or emergency medical personnel, that the person is on a bad batch of LSD. That way, they'd know exactly how to help.

HOW TO KILL A TRIP - A MUST HAVE IN A PSYCHONAUT'S DRUG KIT

A trip killer is any substance that you would take with the intention of ending a psychedelic experience. If you are a psychonaut, it's highly recommended to have trip killers in your drug kit as you never know whether or not you'll have a bad trip that could endanger your safety.

Disclaimer: This is not medical advice and the information I am about to offer you is based on my own experiences and on research I've done on the topic. This is general information, so it's ultimately up to you to do further research to find out the exact dosages you'll need to take to end a trip.

We will discuss: Various substances that you can use to kill bad trips; How they work; Any negative side effects that they may have; Any precautions that you may need to take.

Safety warning: When using trip killers, you need to practice harm reduction procedures before you ingest or inject any substance. You have to test your trip killers to ensure that they are not contaminated with fentanyl or carfentanil (this is especially important if you bought them off the street). There is a fentanyl epidemic right now because dealers like to add it to pretty much all kinds of controlled substances to make them seem more potent. Fentanyl is very dangerous: for your own safety, you need to get a fentanyl test kit and use it to test, not just your trip killers, but also every mind-altering substance that you get off the street.

When to take a trip killer

Ideally, I'd recommend against taking a trip killer merely because you are having a bad trip. Psychedelic experiences are supposed to open up our minds and that includes revealing to us the darker parts of our psyche. From a spiritual point of view, a bad trip is just as beneficial as a good one. Bad trips can reveal the things that trouble you so that you can work on them in service of personal growth.

However, you should absolutely take a trip killer in cases where a bad trip could be a potential risk to your safety. In rare cases, bad trips can turn into terror trips or full-on waking nightmares. There are many reports of people harming themselves or ending their own lives because they are trapped in terror trips. Since psychedelics tend to warp time and reality, it could get to a point where you feel that death is the only escape. In such cases, having trip killers in your drug kit could literally save your life.

Here are the most effective trip killers:

Benzodiazepines

They are some of the most common and most effective trip killers. They are also the kinds that are used by doctors in emergency situations; if you show up at the ER with symptoms of psychosis, you will most likely be given an injection or an oral dose of benzodiazepine.

Benzodiazepines are thought to boost the effects of GABA in the brain and they calm down the nervous system. The exact working mechanism of these types of trip killers is not known, but researchers believe that they attach to the GABA receptors in the brain, and reduce the "excitatory" effects of whatever psychedelic is in your system.

All types of benzodiazepines have the ability to kill trips. However, there are those that are more readily available in the open market than others. Popular benzodiazepines include:

- **Lorazepam** (also called Ativan)
- **Diazepam** (also called Valium)
- **Xanax** (also called Alprazolam)
- **Klonopin** (also called Clonazepam)

In most cases, these benzodiazepines are interchangeable. You can use any one of them to kill any trip. However, there are some important differences that can help you decide which type you might want to acquire:

- Lorazepam and Xanax are the fast-acting types of benzodiazepines.
- Overall, Xanax is the fastest of the bunch.
  However, it's also the shortest-lasting of the group. Its effects only last four to six hours.
- Lorazepam can last up to eight hours.
- Diazepam is the longest-acting; its effects can last more than twelve hours, so it can technically outlast psychedelics such as LSD.
- Based on personal subjective experience, I believe that Lorazepam is the most effective; a small dose

is enough, not just to kill the trip, but to put you to sleep.
- Diazepam will get you out of a bad hallucination, but some of the psychedelic effects will linger on. It's a great choice if you want to eliminate the horrific aspects of your trip, but you still want to enjoy the basic things, e.g., the visual patterns.
- If you swallow Diazepam tablets, it can take a while for their effects to kick in. To get it to work faster, you should chew the tablet and then put some of the crushed bits under your tongue so that it's absorbed sublingually.

The effectiveness of the benzodiazepine (or any other type of trip killer) will depend on:

- The dose of the trip killer.
- At what point during your trip you take the trip killer. For example, if you take the trip killer when the psychedelic effects are at their peak, it would be less effective, and you might need to up your dosage.
- Your biological factors, e.g., age, gender, weight, drug use history (if you've used the drug in the past, you tend to build a tolerance, and it would be less effective).

Here's what to expect when you take a benzodiazepine trip killer:

- On average, most people tend to take trip killers about three hours into their psychedelic trips; it's at this point that things tend to get really intense, so that's when terror trips are most likely to get overwhelming.

- At that point, you would take a benzodiazepine (preferably in tablet form), chew it, and swish it around your mouth to hasten the absorption rate, then swallow it.
- Soon after you swallow, the placebo effect would kick in, and you'll start feeling a little better because you know that the trip will end soon enough.
- A quarter of an hour after taking the trip killer, you feel a wave of relaxation. If you were restless before, you are likely to sit or lie down calmly at this point.
- Half to three-quarters of an hour after taking the trip killer, you would notice that the visual aspects of your trip have either reduced or they have levelled off.
- An hour after taking the trip killer, the visuals, and all other psychedelic effects, would have virtually disappeared.
- Two to three hours after taking the trip killer, you would either be totally sober, or you would have fallen asleep. The only noticeable effects at this point would be that things may appear brighter than usual.

Benzodiazepines and addiction

You should avoid benzodiazepines if you have an addictive personality in general, or worse yet if you have a specific history of benzodiazepine abuse: Benzodiazepines are extremely addictive. They have very long withdrawal periods, the longest of any kind of drugs. Once you are hooked on benzodiazepines, quitting is extremely difficult; withdrawal symptoms are so intense, they could lead to seizure or death. Benzodiazepines become even more addictive when they cut with fentanyl.

Antipsychotic medications

After benzodiazepines, antipsychotic medications are the second most effective substances when it comes to ending psychedelic trips. Ordinarily, they are used to treat conditions such as schizophrenia, bipolar disorder, and other similar conditions, so they are specifically developed to control psychotic symptoms such as hallucinations. These medications are hard to find on the street because they are highly controlled and there isn't such a big market for them.

Common trip killers in this category include:

- **Seroquel**
- **Zyprexa**

Other less-common trip killers

There are some other substances (both controlled and legal) that have shown some promise when it comes to killing trips. They include:

- **Etizolam**, which is a research chemical that is closely related to benzodiazepine. Being a research chemical, it's possible to acquire it legally in some countries.
- **Phenibut** is a nootropic chemical that is somewhat similar to benzodiazepines in effect. The caveat is that it takes between two and four hours for it to kick in, which means that although relief will come eventually, you will be stuck in the bad trip for a while. There are cases where this

nootropic has been known to induce seizures when used with certain types of psychedelics. Don't use it unless you do thorough research first and you are assured of your safety.
- **Antidepressants** (e.g., trazodone) are also effective in killing trips.
- **Alcohol**: Some people use alcohol to kill trips. It has been known to work in some cases, but it is not very effective. It could, however, be safer than benzodiazepines because it is relatively less addictive. Using alcohol as a trip killer can be very uncomfortable because psychedelics heighten your senses, so when you drink alcohol when you are tripping, you get a very strong burning sensation, which could technically worsen a bad trip.

Finally

Before you resort to using your trip killer, make sure that you have exhausted all your other options. When you start having a bad trip, you should first try meditation, breathing exercises, talking to someone, and listening to soothing music. Only use your trip killer when you sense that you can't get your feelings of panic under control.

ALSO BY ALEX GIBBONS

Did you enjoy the book or learn something new? It really helps out small publishers like Alex if you could leave a quick review on Amazon so others in the community can also find the book!

———

Want to chill and experience the benefits of mindfulness? Want to do something productive while watching random videos on YouTube?

Get this fun stoner themed coloring book to scribble on for your next trip. Search for 'Alex Gibbons Stoner Coloring Book' on Amazon to get yours now!

———

Thinking about taking other magical drugs? Ever wondered what exactly happens when you take them? Want to make sure you don't have a bad trip?

If you want to read more about the history, origins and effects of Magic Mushrooms, LSD/Acid or DMT, search for 'The Psychedelic Bible' on Amazon!

For daily posts on all things Psychedelic, follow us on Instagram @Psychedelic.curiosity

www.ingramcontent.com/pod-product-compliance
Lightning Source LLC
Chambersburg PA
CBHW021131080526
44587CB00012B/1239